101 FACTS ABOUT
LONGLEAT'S
AMAZING ANIMALS

Published by First Stone Publishing,
an imprint of Corpus Publishing Limited,
Unit 4/5 The Marina, Harbour Road, Lydney,
Gloucestershire, GL15 5ET,
United Kingdom.

Design: Sarah Williams

First Published 2003
Text and design © 2003 CORPUS PUBLISHING LIMITED
Photography © 2003 LONGLEAT ENTERPRISES LIMITED

ALL RIGHTS RESERVED

No part of this publication may be reproduced in any material form, whether by photocopying, scanning, down-loading onto computer or otherwise without the written permission of the copyright owners, except in accordance with the Copyright, Designs and Patents Act 1988. Applications should be addressed in the first instance, in writing, to the Publisher. Any unauthorised or restricted act in relation to this publication may result in civil proceedings and/or criminal prosecution.

ISBN 1 904439 08 X

Printed in Hong Kong through Printworks Int. Ltd

0 9 8 7 6 5 4 3 2 1

Longleat belongs to the 7th Marquess of Bath, and the magnificent 3,500 hectare estate has become home to some of the world's most spectacular animals.

This was the first drive-through wildlife safari park to be developed outside Africa, and it has given us the unique opportunity to see animals such as lions and tigers roaming free within their huge enclosures. Giraffe and zebra graze side by side, monkeys forage for food and, in the shade of the trees, the wolves rear their pups.

Longleat is also playing a major role in conservation, breeding animals such as the White Rhinoceros, which are in great danger of becoming extinct in the wild.

101 Facts About LONGLEAT'S AMAZING ANIMALS

1 The **Lion** – the King of the Jungle – is the most famous animal at Longleat. Longleat has two prides, which are kept apart from each other.

2 Lions live in family groups called prides and they like to keep to their own special territory.

3 A male Lion will roar to warn off intruders – a sound that can be heard at a distance of 5 miles.

4 In the wild, the Lions stalk their prey, moving up step by step and then catching their victim with one explosive burst of speed. The lion, with his magnificent mane, can be easily spotted, so the lionesses do most of the hunting.

6 At Longleat, a meat wagon is driven through the enclosures to encourage the Lions to 'chase' their food.

5 Even when food is plentiful, there may be a kill only once every 3-4 days. So, a Lion will gorge himself when food is available. A Lion has been known to eat 43 kg (95 lb) at a single sitting!

7 Lions believe in taking life easy – they will generally sleep for 16-20 hours every day.

8 The **Tiger** is the largest member of the big cat family and, unlike the sociable lion, he prefers to live and hunt on his own.

9 At Longleat, you will see the Bengal Tiger, which comes from India. The female Tiger (below) has rare 'white' colouring. This colour is now extinct in the wild.

10 Tiger stripes are like human fingerprints – no two Tigers have the same markings.

11 The mighty Tiger can be as silent as a mouse when he is stalking his prey. If a man covered a distance of 137 m (450 ft) as slowly and quietly as possible, it would take 2 minutes. When a Tiger is hunting, it would take him 15 minutes to cover the same distance.

101 Facts About LONGLEAT'S AMAZING ANIMALS

12 The Tiger uses his sharp, ferocious-looking teeth to kill his prey. His front teeth (upper canines) are the largest of all big cats, measuring the size of a man's middle finger.

Despite the Tiger's great skill and cunning, only 1 in 10 hunts will be successful.

13 Tigers are the only big cats that love water. A Tiger can swim without difficulty across a river that is 4 miles wide.

14 A Tigress has 2-3 cubs in a litter and looks after them on her own until they are 2 years old and ready to find their own territory.

101 Facts About LONGLEAT'S AMAZING ANIMALS

15 The **Rhinoceros** is one of the most ancient creatures in the animal kingdom. There were rhinos living on earth 40 million years ago.

16 At Longleat, you will see the White Rhinoceros, which comes from Africa. This is one of the heaviest of all animals – weighing up to 2 tonnes (2205 lb).

17 The White Rhino has two horns. The horns are made out of keratin – the same material that fingernails are made of.

18 Powdered Rhino horn is highly valued in Chinese Medicine, so thousands of Rhinos have been killed for their horn. In the last 30 years the number of Rhinos living in the wild has dropped by 80 per cent.

101 Facts About LONGLEAT'S AMAZING ANIMALS

19 The Rhino has very poor eyesight. If you were only 30.5 m (100 ft) away from a Rhino and standing still, he probably wouldn't see you!

20 On a hot day the Rhino loves to wallow in a muddy pool. The 'mud coat' protects his hide (skin) from insect bites.

21 Females and their calves live in a group, which is known as a crash. You often see females having friendly nose-rubbing sessions. Males live on their own and they fight fiercely if another male enters their territory.

22 When you see a **Zebra** and **Giraffe** grazing side by side at Longleat, you can really imagine you are in an African game reserve.

23 The Giraffe is the tallest animal on earth, reaching a height of some 4-5 m (13-16 ft).

24 The Giraffe uses his long neck to reach the leaves at the top of trees. Watch out for his huge tongue, which measures around 45 cm (18 in).

25 For such a tall, ungainly animal, the Giraffe can move surprisingly

101 Facts About LONGLEAT'S AMAZING ANIMALS

fast. He has a top speed of 35 miles per hour.

26 When adult bull (male) Giraffes fight over females, they 'arm-wrestle' with each other by entwining their necks.

27 Every family of Zebra has its own coat markings – and no two Zebras are alike. At Longleat, you will see Grants Zebra.

28 The Zebra is a prey animal, which means that he must always be on the look-out for meat-eating predators.

29 The Zebra finds safety in numbers and grazes in big herds.

30 There are three reasons for the Zebra's striped coat. Firstly, it makes it difficult for a predator to pick out a single animal from the herd and secondly, it helps keep flies at bay. Finally, members of the Zebra herd recognise each other by their stripes.

32 The Rhesus Monkey comes from Asia and lives in forests, eating fruit and insects and foraging on the forest floor (where it is cooler) for leaves and roots.

33 These Monkeys have special cheek pouches, in which they can stuff as much as a day's food supply.

31 The **Rhesus Monkey** is Longleat's most inquisitive animal. If you stop your car, you could have Monkeys coming to investigate.

34 At Longleat, food is scattered around the Monkey Jungle, so

101 Facts About LONGLEAT'S AMAZING ANIMALS

the Monkeys have to forage, just as they would in the wild.

35 Rhesus Monkeys live in troops of 20-150 adult females, youngsters and babies, plus several adult males.

36 It is easy to tell how a Rhesus Monkey is feeling – just watch his face!

His expressions include an angry stare, a frightened grin and a special yawn which shows off all his teeth.

37 Babies are born at night. A mother needs to keep on the move, so the baby clings on to the hair of her stomach with his hands and feet.

38 In the wild, Rhesus Monkeys sleep in trees. At Longleat, they have their own purpose-built housing but most prefer to sleep in holes within the 300-year-old trees in their enclosure.

39 You will have to keep your eyes wide open in Wolf Wood, as the Canadian **Timber Wolves** like to seek the shade of the trees.

40 In the wild, Wolves live in packs, which are ruled by the top male and female, known as the alpha male and female. They are the only pair that will breed in the pack.

41 At Longleat, the alpha male and female have lighter coloured coats. When they have a litter, the other pack members will help to look after the pups.

42 The Timber Wolf, also known as the Grey Wolf, is quite a big animal, measuring up to 81 cm (32 in) at the shoulder but its success as a hunter comes from working in a team.

43 A pack of Wolves hunting together can bring down a moose weighing 10 times more than a single Wolf!

44 The pack has great powers of endurance when it is hunting and can keep going for 24 hours, maintaining a steady speed of 28 miles per hour.

45 The Wolf howls to keep in touch with other members of the pack. Sometimes the pack will meet together and howl in unison – an eerie chorus that can be heard more than 6 miles away.

101 Facts About LONGLEAT'S AMAZING ANIMALS

46 There are animals at Longleat that are in danger of becoming extinct in the wild. Breeding programmes play a major part in helping these animals to survive.

47 **Pere David Deer** (pictured below) were once found in large numbers in the swampy plains of northern China – but became extinct in the wild.

48 There are about 700 Pere David Deer that are kept in zoos and wildlife parks and a number of deer, including some from Longleat, have been reintroduced to the wild.

49 The **Scimitar-Horned Oryx** (pictured right) comes from the dry grasslands surrounding the Sahara Desert in Africa. These beautiful

51 Longleat has a herd of female Scimitar-Horned Oryx and it is hoped that they will be used for breeding in the future.

creatures were hunted and driven away from their home land when it was needed for farming.

50 Just before the Oryx became extinct, a group of 41 was caught and protected as a breeding herd. Now several thousand Scimitar-Horned Oryx are kept in zoos and wildlife parks around the world.

52 The **Bactrian Camel** – that's the Camel with two humps – comes from the Gobi Desert, which is in China and Mongolia.

101 Facts About LONGLEAT'S AMAZING ANIMALS

53 It is estimated that there are only around 1,000 Bactrian Camels (pictured right and below) remaining in the wild.

54 It is very cold in the Gobi Desert. The Bactrian Camel has a thick, woolly coat, which it sheds during the summer months. This is why the Bactrian camels at Longleat sometimes look a bit ragged.

55 The Camel can survive in very harsh conditions, where there is very little food and scarcely any water.

56 They can eat the thorniest plants and they store fat in their humps, which can be used as a food supply in times of need.

57 Camels can go for months without drinking water, and then they can drink 200 litres (352 pints) in a single day, which would kill any other animal.

58 **Tapirs** (pictured right) have been on earth for 55 million years – even longer than the ancient Rhinoceros – but now they are under threat in the wild.

59 They live in dense forest areas, sniffing out roots and plants with their snout-like noses. When in danger they take to the water and they can stay under the surface for several minutes.

60 At Longleat, you will see the South American Tapir. The young are born with a spotted and striped coat to blend in with their surroundings.

61 The **Asiatic Water Buffalo** (above) wins the prize for the longest horns of any animal at Longleat – they can grow up to 4 m (13 ft) from tip to tip.

62 In India, Water Buffalo are highly valued because they produce large quantities of rich milk, and they can also be used to plough the rice paddy fields.

63 The **Common Eland** (pictured right) comes from Africa and can be recognised by its long, spiral horns. A female has been known to stab a Lion with her horns when she is protecting her young.

64 It is easy for hunters to detect when a male Eland is about. Their knees make a clicking noise when they walk, which can be heard from a distance of 100 m (328 ft).

65 In South America, the **Llama** (pictured right) has to contend with the cold climate of the Andes Mountains and so he has a huge woolly coat to keep him warm.

66 Llamas are kept in big herds for their wool and also to carry heavy loads. You had better watch out if a Llama gets angry – he will bite and kick. He can also spit out food from his stomach – yuck!

21

67 If you want to experience what it feels like to live in the hot tropical regions of the world, you should head for the Longleat **Butterfly** Garden.

68 Hundreds of different types of tropical Butterflies are kept in temperatures of 26 degrees Celsius (80 F), flying in their own jungle of tropical plants and flowers.

69 Most are brightly coloured but some, like the Owl Butterfly (pictured above right), blend in with their surroundings.

70 The Butterflies you see have gone through some amazing life changes before emerging as beautiful creatures.

71 The female Butterfly will lay her eggs on a leaf, making sure that there is a good supply of food nearby.

72 The eggs hatch and a Caterpillar emerges. Caterpillars are great feeders. As they get bigger, they shed or moult their skin to make room for their growing bodies.

73 When the Caterpillar is fully grown, it will transform itself into a pupa (pictured below). In time, the case of the pupa will crack and a Butterfly will emerge.

74 The place to get close to the animals is Pets Corner. You may even get the chance to touch one!

75 You can see some animals that you might keep at home, such as **Rabbits**, **Guinea Pigs**, and cuddly-looking **Chinchillas**.

76 But you can also see some more exotic creatures, such as the **Green Iguana** (pictured above), which comes from South America. This beautifully coloured reptile is only about 18 cm (7 in) long when he is born, but he can grow to a length of 2 m (6.5 ft).

77 The **Royal Python** (pictured below) may look menacing but in fact this snake is quite shy and will curl into a ball, which is why he is also known as the Ball Python.

78 The noisiest animal in Pets Corner is the **Blue and Gold Macaw** (pictured above). This highly intelligent bird can learn stunts and is also a good mimic.

79 The **Otter** is a born entertainer, and Longleat's Asian Short-Clawed Otters (pictured below) put on a great show, playing in their enclosure.

80 They are as much at home in the water as on land. An Otter has a waterproof coat and webbed paws. It can close off its nostrils to stay underwater for 4-5 minutes.

The Ugh! Show

81 You love them or you hate them – but everyone is fascinated by the creepy crawlies in "The Ugh! Show".

82 The **Chilean Rose Tarantula** Spider (pictured below) is a fierce hunter, ambushing its prey and then biting down on its victim.

83 Female Tarantulas can live for 30 years, but most males are lucky to reach their sixth birthday. Many die after mating because of the injuries inflicted by the females!

84 The **Giant African Land Snail** (pictured above right) is huge compared with most Snails. The biggest ever recorded measured 40 cm (16 in) from snout to tail and weighed 0.9 kg (2 lb).

Death's Head Cockroach (pictured below), which is named after its skull and vampire face markings.

87 A Cockroach can live for a week without its head – it only dies because it cannot drink water!

85 The Giant African Land Snail has a huge appetite and will eat 500 different types of plant. It lays 1,200 eggs a year, so in no time an area can become overun with Snails.

86 At Longleat, you may see the

88 Before you board the boat for Longleat's water safari, stop and look at the **Meerkats** (pictured left), which live alongside the Half Mile Lake.

89 Meerkats are insect-eating mammals that live in large groups in hot, dry areas of Africa. They dig burrows underground, and come out to hunt for food in the cool of the evening.

90 When they are above ground, one of the group acts as guard, and gives a shrill bark if danger approaches.

91 Half Mile Lake is home to Longleat's Californian **Sea Lions** (pictured below). This is a freshwater lake, so Longleat's Sea Lions have salt tablets to keep them healthy.

101 Facts About LONGLEAT'S AMAZING ANIMALS

92 Each Sea Lion is given 4-7 kg (8.8-15.5 lb) of mackerel every day, but Longleat's Sea Lions also catch fresh fish in the lake. They have a particular liking for eels.

93 Unlike Seals, Sea Lions have ear flaps, which they can close when they go underwater. Their spectacular whiskers are used to find food, as they can detect movement in the water when fish are swimming close by.

94 In the wild, the **Hippopotamus** spends 18 hours a day in the water, so the Half Mile Lake and its banks provide a perfect home for Longleat's two Hippos (pictured below).

centrally heated home with satellite TV!

97 Gorillas cannot swim and so the lake provides a secure barrier, allowing the Gorillas to roam free on the island.

95 In their native home, African Hippos only leave the water at night, to come out on to the banks to graze.

98 These huge apes live mostly on a vegetarian diet. Their food is left for them to forage for, as they would in the wild.

96 The island in the middle of the lake is home to Longleat's two **Western Lowland Gorillas**. They have all the mod cons – including a

99 The Lowland Gorilla lives in a family group of around 12 members made up of females, youngsters, and immature black-back males. The group is led by a mature silver-back male.

100 Gorillas communicate with each other using a series of grunts and hoots and by beating their chests. They are gentle, peace-loving animals, and very rarely fight.

101 Seeing the Gorillas roaming free on their island is one of the many highspots of visiting Longleat. By watching the animals, we can learn more about them and, by supporting Longleat, we can help to save a number of species that are threatened with extinction.

101 Facts About LONGLEAT'S AMAZING ANIMALS

FIND THE CREATURE....

You will find the answers to these seven questions in this book.
To give you a clue where to look, we have told you what page to read again.
Write your answer in the space provided.

1. Original home of the white rhinocerous (page 8) – – – – – –

2. The king of the jungle (page 4) – – – –

3. Woolly animal from South America (page 21) – – – – –

4. This reptile can grow and grow! (page 24) – – – – – –

5. Type of monkey (page 12) – – – – – –

6. Creature with sharp horns (page 16) – – – –

7. Tallest animal at Longleat (page 10) – – – – – – –

When you have answered all the questions, take the first letter of each answer and write it in the spaces below to make a new word.

– – – – – – –

Now read it BACKWARDS to find the missing animal!

(Answers below)

Answers: 1. Africa; 2. Lion; 3. Llama; 4. Iguana; 5. Rhesus; 6. Oryx; 7. Giraffe. Missing animal: Gorilla.